Writing B1

The Ultimate PET Writing Guide for B1 Cambridge

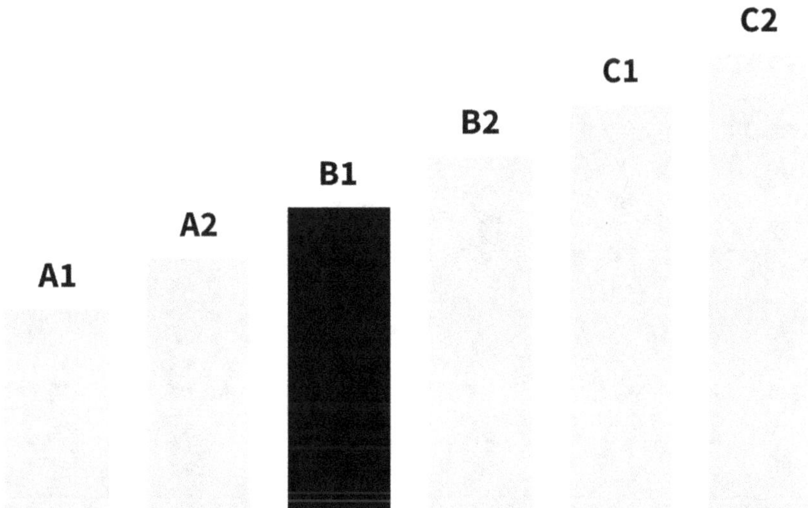

KSE Academy®

Luis Porras Wadley

KSE Academy®

Granada, Spain

First published in January 2023

ISBN: 9788409475056

Manufactured on demand by Kindle Direct Publishing.

For further information and resources, please visit: kseacademy.com

Disclaimer

Cambridge B1 Preliminary and PET are brands belonging to The University of Cambridge and are not associated with KSE Academy or the author of this work.

Table of Contents

Table of Contents

Introduction

Welcome to *Writing B1: The Ultimate PET Writing Guide for B1 Cambridge*.

This guide covers the main writing tasks that appear in the Cambridge Assessment English examination B1 Preliminary, previously known as the Preliminary English Test (PET). These tasks are emails, articles and stories.

This book provides six sample tasks and answers for each type of writing, plus a whole set of useful expressions for each type of task that candidates can use in their writing. Ideally, students should use these samples as models for their own writing tasks, making use of the helpful phrases provided at the end of each section.

Besides the sample tasks and useful expressions, this guide also contains a description of Writing Part 1 and Writing Part 2, a full description of every task type, answers to candidates' frequently asked questions (FAQ), guidance on developing an appropriate writing strategy, a description of how writing is assessed and a sample mark sheet which can be used to assess students' performance or as a self-assessment tool.

This writing guide is aimed at students of English as a foreign language who are interested in improving their writing skills with a view to obtaining their B1 Preliminary certificate, and at teachers who want support writing material to use with their own students.

About the author

Luis Porras Wadley is the owner and director of KSE Academy, an online English academy and official Cambridge Exam Preparation Centre based in Granada. As an English teacher, Luis has been preparing Cambridge candidates successfully for more than ten years. He is the author of other successful test preparation books, including *The Ultimate B2 First Writing Guide, The Ultimate CAE Writing Guide for C1 Cambridge, Speaking First, Speaking CAE and Speaking CPE*, among others.

B1 Writing: Level Description by the CEFRL

The B1 Preliminary certifies a B1 level of proficiency as described by the Common European Framework of Reference for Languages (CEFRL), which corresponds to a lower-intermediate level of English.

According to the CEFRL, someone at the B1 level, in general:

"Can produce simple connected texts on topics which are familiar or of personal interest. Can describe experiences and events, dreams, hopes and ambitions and briefly give reasons and explanations for opinions and plans." (CEFRL, p. 24)

If we dig deeper into the B1 level, we see that an English learner at the B1 level in writing:

In overall written production:

"Can write straightforward connected texts on a range of familiar subjects within his/her field of interest, by linking a series of shorter discrete elements into a linear sequence." (CEFRL, p. 61)

In creative writing:

"Can write straightforward, detailed descriptions on a range of familiar subjects within his/her field of interest. Can write accounts of experiences, describing feelings and reactions in simple connected text. Can write a description of an event, a recent trip – real or imagined. Can narrate a story." (CEFRL, p. 62)

In reports and essays:

"Can write short, simple essays on topics of interest. Can summarise, report and give his/her opinion about accumulated factual information on familiar routine and non-routine matters within his/her field with some confidence. Can write very brief reports to a standard conventionalised format, which pass on routine factual information and state reasons for actions." (CEFRL, p. 62)

As you can see, everything a B1 candidate produces in writing is expected to be about familiar topics, topics of personal interest, their own opinion, familiar subjects, etc. And some keywords stand out in these level descriptions. For example, *straightforward, simple, brief, short*, etc. This means that these texts are not expected to be very complex, as we might expect at higher levels like B2 or, certainly, at C1 and C2 levels.

B1 Preliminary: Writing

In the B1 Preliminary Writing paper, candidates have to prove that they can write different types of texts in English using linguistic resources which show that they have a B1 level of written English. There are two parts in the Writing component, and they have 45 minutes to complete both parts.

B1 Preliminary: Writing Part 1

What's in Writing Part 1?

Candidates are provided with an email they have received. The email is annotated with a set of prompts presented as notes. All of this gives candidates the context, who they are writing to and why, and four key content points. Candidates have to read and interpret the email and respond to it accordingly. In their answer, they must include the four content points in a response of around 100 words.

The goal of this email in Part 1 is to allow candidates to demonstrate the skill to use functional language, which might include agreeing and disagreeing, giving their opinion, offering to do something and explaining something to the target reader.

Candidates' emails should be well organised, containing all the necessary structural elements expected in emails, and they should cover the four key points highlighted in the instructions. They ought to read every part of the task carefully and not omit any required development of the topic.

What do candidates need to practise?

Using language functions, such as agreeing, disagreeing, giving an opinion, offering, explaining, reacting to information, etc.

How many tasks are there?

There is only one compulsory task in Part 1, which is always an email.

How many words do candidates have to write?

About 100 words

B1 Preliminary: Writing Part 2

What's in part 2?

Candidates have to write a text from a choice of two text types: article or story. These different types of tasks are designed to provide situations and contexts in which candidates can put together and develop their ideas on a subject, with a specific purpose for writing, target reader and context in mind. As guidance, candidates are given some information about the context, the topic, the purpose, and the target reader.

For the article, candidates are provided with a snippet from a magazine or website, usually an announcement, and they must write about it responding to the information provided. For the story, candidates are provided with the first sentence of the story, so they need to develop the rest of the story based on the first sentence.

For an appropriate response, candidates must pay attention to every aspect of the question, and they must use language that is appropriate for the task. For example, in the story task, it is important to pay attention to the pronouns used in the first sentence, as it will determine the approach of the rest of the task.

What do students need to practise?

Writing different types of text that could come up in the exam, focusing on the style and structure of the different task types as well as different language functions.

How many tasks are there?

There are two tasks in Part 2, but candidates must do only one.

How many words do candidates have to write?

About 100 words

Candidates' FAQ

How many tasks do I have to write?

You will have to write two tasks, as there are two parts. In the first part, you will have to write an email. In the second part, you will have to choose one task from a choice of two: an article or a story.

What if I write too much (over 100 words) or too little (under 100 words)?

Cambridge writing assessors do not count how many words you have written to determine whether to penalise you or not. But you must consider the following: if you have written a lot more words than necessary, you have probably included irrelevant information in the task. In the same way, if you fall very short, you are probably lacking essential information. Those two things would affect your grade negatively. For this reason, I always recommend not obsessing over the number of words and focusing instead on tackling every single point of the task effectively. And, if you still want to set yourself a hard limit, I would limit writing tasks to 10–20 words under or over the recommended limit. That way, you have slightly more freedom to write but are still constrained by a reasonable limit.

How long can I spend on each task?

Both tasks have the same word limit, are similar in difficulty, and are worth the same number of marks. For this reason, given that you have 45 minutes to do both tasks, I recommend spending up to 20 minutes on the first one, so that you have at least another 25 minutes for the second one.

Where do I have to write my answers?

If you are taking a computer-based test, you must write your answers on the computer just like the rest of the test. In this case, you are also provided, if you wish, with rough paper to make some notes.

If you are doing a paper-based test, you will have to write your answers in the answer booklet, which is provided to you at the beginning of the writing component. Also, if you need more paper, you can request it from the supervisor or invigilator of the exam session. But make sure that at the end of the exam, you turn in all of the papers with your final answers and nothing else.

When writing the story, do I need to include the first sentence in my text?

Yes, you do. The instructions clearly say *"Your story must begin with this sentence"*. Therefore, you must include it. Your text must be able to be read without the instructions and it probably would not make sense without the first sentence.

Does the first sentence in a story count towards the number of words?

Yes, it does. Everything you write will count towards the number of words, including the first sentence. However, as explained on the previous page, you should focus on responding appropriately to the instructions, and not so much on the number of words.

When writing an email, do I need to include an email address or other sender/recipient details?

No, you don't. Writing an email address is not necessary and, if you do write it, you will be wasting time and space. As regards sender or recipient details, it is enough to write the recipient's name at the beginning and sign with your name at the end.

Can I use a pencil for a paper-based exam?

No, you can't. You must do this part using a pen. You can use a pencil, if you wish, to write a draft on a different sheet of paper, but not on the answer booklet. Just in case, I recommend not even having a pencil on the table while doing the Writing component.

What if I'm using a pencil instead of a pen in the exam?

In this case, you need to tell your exam supervisor as soon as possible so they can give you another answer booklet. You will need to copy over using a pen whatever you have written. However, you will not have extra time to do so.

Can I repeat exact phrases from the instructions in my answers?

While you can, and sometimes it will be natural to do so, you should use your own words as far as possible.

Can I just memorise an email for Writing Part 1?

While you can and should memorise the structural elements of an email, you must not learn a pre-prepared answer, as it will not fit the task in the exam.

Candidates' FAQ (cont.)

Are mistakes allowed in the B1 Preliminary Writing paper?

Mistakes are neither allowed nor forbidden. Cambridge writing examiners will focus on what you can do rather than what you cannot. For this reason, making mistakes does not automatically mean you are bound to fail. Errors which do not affect communication, will not necessarily be penalised. These might include spelling, grammar or punctuation mistakes. However, if they do impede proper communication, they will be treated more severely.

How do spelling and punctuation affect my grade?

Spelling errors and faulty punctuation are not specifically penalised, but you should know that mistakes in these areas can sometimes impede communication and have a negative effect on the target reader's impression. Please double-check your writing to avoid these errors before submitting it.

In paper-based exams, do I need to write everything in capital letters?

No, you don't. The use of capital letters might be compulsory in other parts of the exam, but not in the writing paper. If you do, it will not be a problem, but you will probably be more comfortable using lower-case handwriting.

My handwriting is not very good. What should I do?

The quality of your handwriting is not assessed in the test. The important thing is that your text is easily legible. If your handwriting is so bad that other people cannot read it, you might have to make an effort to make it clearer when doing the exam or you can consider doing the exam in its computer-based format.

Am I allowed to underline the task instructions?

Yes, you are. You are encouraged to do so. If you are doing a paper-based exam, simply use your pen to underline whatever you want. If you are doing a computer-based exam, you can select the text you wish to underline, then right-click using your mouse or trackpad and highlight it. In this case, the text will appear in yellow.

Can I use a dictionary during the exam?

No, you can't. Dictionaries are not allowed in the B1 Preliminary examination.

Can I take some notes with me after the writing exam?

No, you can't. You are not allowed to take with you any of the test materials or rough paper used during the exam. The supervisor or invigilator will collect those before you leave the exam room.

I would like to revise my writing at home. Can I take a copy with me after the test?

No, you can't. Just like you cannot take your notes with you, you are not allowed to take with you any copy or rough paper used during the exam. The supervisor or invigilator will collect those before you leave the exam room.

Is American English spelling incorrect?

No, not at all. Any standard spelling variety will be considered correct, whether it be in British English or American English. So you can write "realise" or "realize", for instance. However, even though this does not affect your score, you should be consistent with your spelling and stick to one variety as far as possible.

In Part 1, do I have to write about all the points highlighted in the email?

Yes, you do. Those are called key content points and must be addressed clearly in your writing. But remember that you should use your own words as far as possible.

Can I use bold font, italics or underline when doing a computer-based test?

No, you can't. The text you write is plain text. You can, however, use capital letters for headings if you want them to stand out.

Emails

Writing Part 1: Emails

Purpose of an email

Given that an email is written in response to a situation outlined in the task, its purpose will depend on each specific task. In general, at this level, the purpose of the email task is usually to react to good or bad news, to agree or disagree with some idea, to explain why you agree or disagree, to respond to questions, to ask for information, to suggest some ideas, etc.

Register

Every email has a particular target reader in mind. At B1 Preliminary, this reader will typically be a friend or a relative. Therefore, standard or informal language is expected. Given that we are dealing with a lower-intermediate level of English, all the situations are familiar, so no formal language is required or expected.

Structure

Every email should have a similar, conventional structure. You need an opening salutation and closing formula; an introductory and closing paragraph; and the main body, which usually consists of as many paragraphs as key points are highlighted in the task email.

Common topics

Many emails to friends and relatives include giving advice on a certain subject like visiting your town, keeping fit, making plans, arranging a trip or a meet-up, etc.

How to Write an Email for B1 Preliminary

In this part of the test, you are given an email from an English-speaking friend or relative, and you are asked to respond to it in about 100 words. This email contains annotations which help you identify exactly what you need to include in your email.

Here's an example:

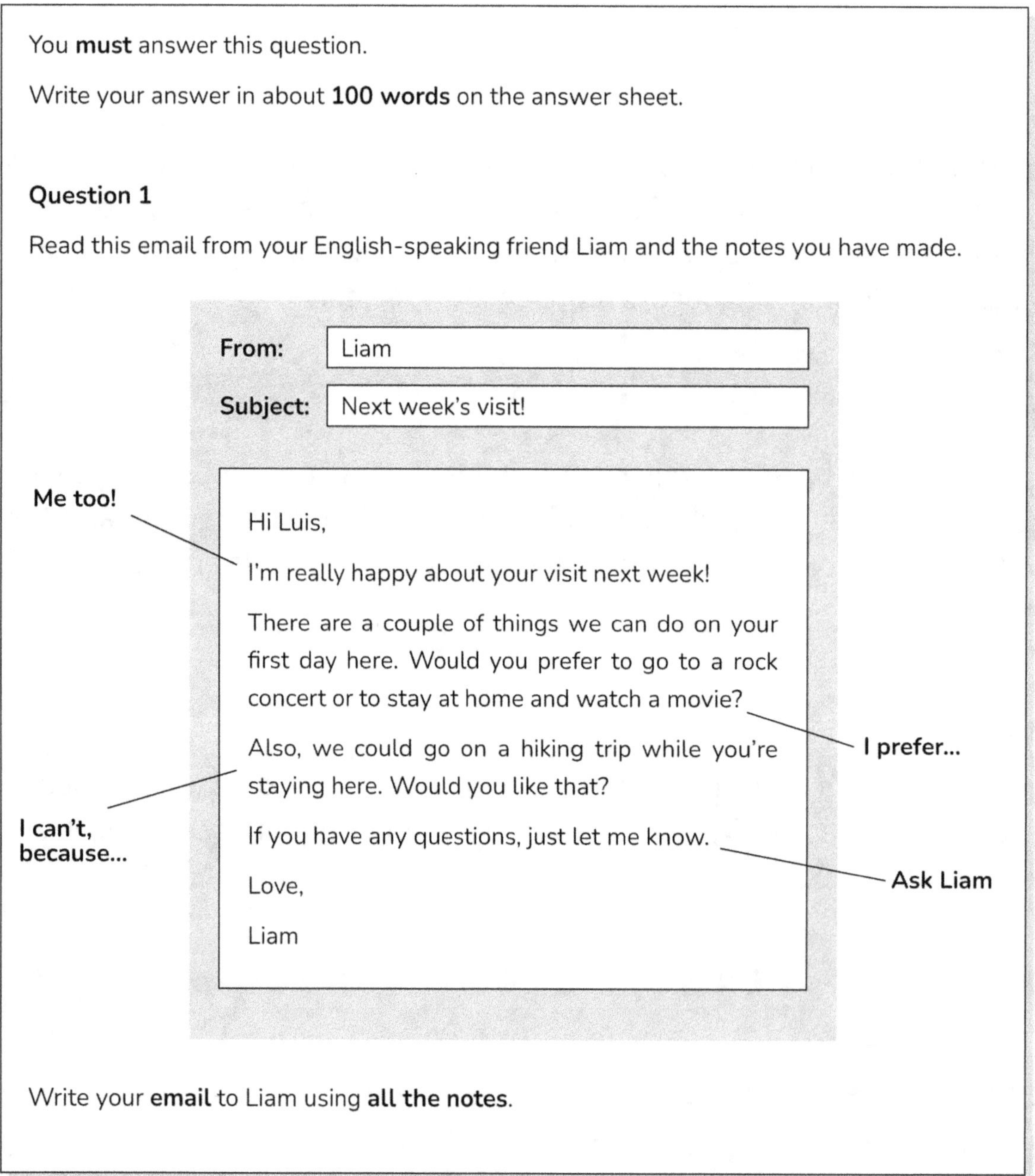

How to Write an Email for B1 Preliminary (cont.)

As you can see in the previous sample task, you have received an email from a person called Liam, who is a friend of yours. In addition, you have made some annotations, which, are the key content points you need to address in your email:

Me too!

I prefer…

I can't, because…

Ask Liam

Having these key content points highlighted has two main purposes:

* Clarify what you must write about.
* Determine how many paragraphs the email will have.

Email Structure

Every email consists of the following parts:

* **Greeting:** Greet the other person (i.e. say *Hi* or *Hello*).
* **Opening paragraph:** React to the other person's news and ask them how they are feeling and whatever else you feel is appropriate.
* **Main paragraphs:** Deal with the key content points, which are highlighted in the instructions.
* **Closing paragraph:** Begin to say goodbye by wishing the other person well and asking them to reply to your email.
* **Goodbye:** Short phrase to say goodbye.
* **Signature:** Sign the email with your name.

In general, all emails must follow the same structure, and also, remember that in Cambridge exams you do not need to write *From:*, *To:* or a subject.

Now that we know the different parts of an email, we should see a sample answer.

How to Write an Email for B1 Preliminary (cont.)

Now let's take a look at the following email, where we can see a sample answer to the task on page 16:

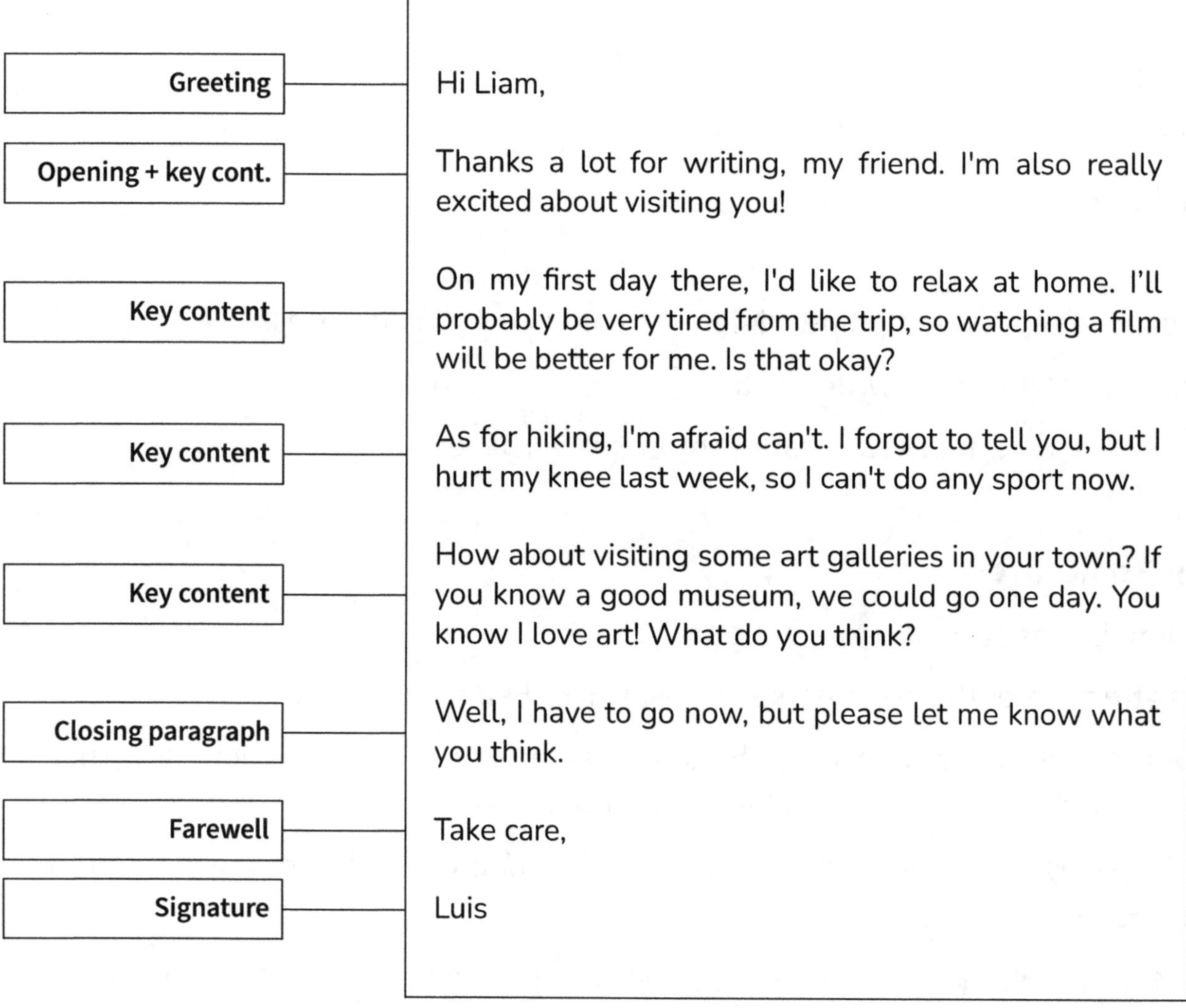

In the example above, you can see that the different parts of an email are very well defined. It is important that your email shows this structure clearly and that your writing is visually appealing, apart from having good grammar and vocabulary.

Your paragraphs should be well defined, leaving a space in between, and you should know when to add line breaks. This is especially important after greetings, after opening and closing paragraphs, and after saying goodbye. This will make your text visually appealing, as it will make it look like a real email.

How to Write an Email for B1 Preliminary (cont.)

Top 5 Tips for writing an Email for B1 Preliminary

Learn and memorise a set of expressions

Make sure you already know a set of expressions to use in your greetings, opening and closing paragraphs, and farewells. This will save you a lot of time while doing a task, and you will avoid making mistakes, as you will already know the expressions by heart.

Write a well-structured and visually-appealing email

One of the things Cambridge English examiners pay attention to is the organisation of your piece of writing, so make sure not to write a messy email. Also, remember that punctuation matters, so be sure to separate your sentences with stops and commas and do not write excessively long sentences.

Brainstorm, write, read and edit

Before starting to write your email, brainstorm a couple of things and write down some ideas. This can include vocabulary related to the topic. For example, if you have to write about TV shows, you can write down things like *contestants*, *cookery show*, *prize*, etc. Then, write out your email. After that, read it and look for possible mistakes or opportunities for improvement (e.g.: adding descriptive adjectives, rephrasing sentences, etc.).

Read carefully and identify what you have to do

Do not start writing right away. Make sure you read the task carefully and that you identify exactly what you are being asked to do. Sometimes, we do not pay attention to the instructions and we end up writing about something different. This will mean losing points.

Experiment at home, be conservative in the exam

Homework is the best chance to get creative and experiment with different ways to express yourself. So make sure you try your hardest to keep improving when you write at home. However, when you're doing an exam, don't risk trying out new words or expressions you are unsure of, as you may be making a mistake. So be conservative in your exam and stick to what you already know works.

Sample Email 1

Instructions

You **must** answer this question.

Write your answer in about **100 words** on the answer sheet.

Question 1

Read this email from your English-speaking friend Katie and the notes you have made.

| From: | Katie |
| Subject: | Your visit next month! |

Me too

Hi Sarah,

I'm excited about your visit next month!

I was thinking we could do a few things while you're here. Would you like to visit the art museum and go to a new sushi restaurant? — Both!

I also thought it might be fun to go for a bike ride along the river trail. Would you be up for that?

I don't like bikes

If you have any other ideas or preferences, just let me know. — Go for a picnic

Looking forward to seeing you,

Katie

Write your **email** to Katie using **all the notes**.

Do you need someone to mark your email for B1?

Check out KSE Academy's writing assessment service. Scan the QR code on the left with your phone or visit *https://kdp.kseacademy.com/writing-b1-book* for more information. Use the coupon *AMZWB1* for a great discount as a thank you for purchasing this book.

Sample Email 1

Answer

Hi Katie,

I'm really excited too. I can't wait to visit!

Both the art museum and sushi restaurant sound like great ideas. As you know, I'm always keen on trying new things, especially food!

Unfortunately, I'm not a fan of bike riding, so I'm afraid I'm not interested in going cycling along the river.

However, I think a picnic would be a lot of fun! It's a nice way to enjoy the beautiful weather and spend time together. Do you agree?

I'm looking forward to seeing you too and having a great time together.

Best,

Sarah

Sample Email 2

Instructions

You **must** answer this question.

Write your answer in about **100 words** on the answer sheet.

Question 1

Read this email from your English-speaking friend Jessica and the notes you have made.

From:	Jessica
Subject:	Anne's birthday

It will be fun

You can decide

Hi Rachel,

I'm so excited about Anne's birthday!

I'm thinking about what present to get her, but I'm not sure what she would like. Maybe a book or some jewellery. What do you think?

Also, where should we celebrate it? I think we could go to that pizza restaurant she's always talking about.

Let me know your thoughts.

Thanks,

Jessica

She's a bookworm

Offer to book a table

Write your **email** to Jessica using **all the notes**.

Do you need someone to mark your email for B1?

Check out KSE Academy's writing assessment service. Scan the QR code on the left with your phone or visit *https://kdp.kseacademy.com/writing-b1-book* for more information. Use the coupon *AMZWB1* for a great discount as a thank you for purchasing this book.

Sample Email 2

Answer

Hi Jessica,

I'm also really excited about Anne's birthday. It's going to be so much fun!

As for the present, I think a book would be a great idea because Anne is such a bookworm. But jewellery is always a nice gift too. So I'm sure she will love whatever we get her. You choose!

The pizza restaurant sounds like an awesome place for the celebration. Shall I call them to book a table? If not, we can try the new Thai restaurant.

What do you think? Hope to hear from you soon.

Best wishes,

Rachel

Sample Email 3

Instructions

You **must** answer this question.

Write your answer in about **100 words** on the answer sheet.

Question 1

Read this email from your English-speaking friend Alice and the notes you have made.

From:	Alice
Subject:	Keeping fit

Don't worry

Hi John,

How are you doing?

I've been feeling a bit out of shape lately and I'm not sure how to get fit again.

Gym is cheaper

I'm thinking I should join a gym or hire a personal trainer. Should I also go on a diet? — **Yes!**

By the way, do you have any recommendations for how to stay motivated?

Keep a training diary

I look forward to hearing your thoughts.

Thanks,

Alice

Write your **email** to Alice using **all the notes**.

Do you need someone to mark your email for B1?

Check out KSE Academy's writing assessment service. Scan the QR code on the left with your phone or visit *https://kdp.kseacademy.com/writing-b1-book* for more information. Use the coupon *AMZWB1* for a great discount as a thank you for purchasing this book.

Sample Email 3

Answer

Hi Alice,

I'm doing fine. Thanks for asking!

Don't worry about feeling out of shape. We all feel like that sometimes, and it's completely normal. To get fit again, I think you should join a gym. It's cheaper than a personal trainer and you can choose what to do. But it's also a good idea to follow a healthy diet to support your fitness goals.

As for motivation, my advice is to keep a training diary. With a diary, you can see your progress and your results, which can be very motivating.

I hope my suggestions are helpful. Let me know if you have any more questions!

Regards,

John

Sample Email 4

Instructions

You **must** answer this question.

Write your answer in about **100 words** on the answer sheet.

Question 1

Read this email from your English-speaking friend Emily and the notes you have made.

From: Emily

Subject: Our trip to Paris

It's my second visit

Hi Sam,

I'm so excited about our trip to Paris next month!

There are so many things to do and see! I was thinking about visiting the Eiffel Tower and Notre Dame Cathedral, and trying some traditional French cuisine. What do you think?

Of course! And...

Also, where are we going to stay? Do you know anyone who lives in Paris?

My dad's friend

I look forward to planning our trip together.

Thanks,

Emily

Thanks for your help

Write your **email** to Emily using **all the notes**.

Do you need someone to mark your email for B1?

Check out KSE Academy's writing assessment service. Scan the QR code on the left with your phone or visit *https://kdp.kseacademy.com/writing-b1-book* for more information. Use the coupon *AMZWB1* for a great discount as a thank you for purchasing this book.

Sample Email 4

Answer

Hello Emily,

You have some great ideas for the trip. This will be my second time in Paris, but it's going to be even better this time!

I definitely agree that the Eiffel Tower and Notre Dame Cathedral should be on our list. I also think we should try some traditional French dishes. And how about visiting some gardens? Believe me, they're amazing!

As for a place to stay, my dad has a friend who lives in Paris. I think we could stay with him. What do you think? I'll ask my dad as well.

Thank you for your help, Emily. I'm looking forward to exploring Paris with you!

All the best,

Sam

Sample Email 5

Instructions

You **must** answer this question.

Write your answer in about **100 words** on the answer sheet.

Question 1

Read this email from your English-speaking teacher Mrs Smith and the notes you have made.

From: Mrs. Smith

Subject: Film club

Students seem to like it

Hi Emily,

I'm glad you're interested in joining the film club!

We have a few spots open for new members. Our meetings are held on Wednesday and Friday, in the afternoons. Are you available then?

Not Fridays, because...

Also, what type of films do you enjoy? Let me know if you want to watch one in particular so I can add it to the list.

Thrillers. I want to watch...

I'm looking forward to having you as a member.

Me too

Thanks,

Mrs Smith

Write your **email** to Mrs Smith using **all the notes**.

Do you need someone to mark your email for B1?

Check out KSE Academy's writing assessment service. Scan the QR code on the left with your phone or visit *https://kdp.kseacademy.com/writing-b1-book* for more information. Use the coupon *AMZWB1* for a great discount as a thank you for purchasing this book.

Sample Email 5

Answer

Dear Mrs Smith,

Thank you for your response about the film club. I'm very excited because other students say they really enjoy it.

I'm busy on Friday afternoons because I have dancing lessons, but I'm available on Wednesdays. Could I just go to the Wednesday sessions?

Regarding the types of films I enjoy, thrillers are my favourite. And I would love to watch "The Choice". I heard it's great. Do you think it will be possible?

I'm looking forward to becoming a member of the film club and participating in the meetings. Thanks again.

Sincerely,

Emily

Useful Phrases for Emails

Sample 1

- *I can't wait to visit!*
- *... sound like great ideas.*
- *... I'm always keen on ...*
- *Unfortunately, ...*
- *... I'm afraid I'm not interested ...*
- *Do you agree?*
- *I'm looking forward to seeing you ...*
- *Best,*

Sample 2

- *As for the present, ...*
- *bookworm*
- *an awesome place*
- *Shall I call them ... ?*
- *Hope to hear from you soon.*
- *Best wishes,*

Sample 3

- *I'm doing fine.*
- *Thanks for asking!*
- *It's always a good idea to ...*
- *support your fitness goals*
- *As for motivation, ...*
- *... my advice is to ...*
- *..., which can be very motivating.*
- *I hope ...*
- *helpful*
- *Let me know if ...*
- *Regards,*

Sample 4

- *... it's doing to be even better ...*
- *I definitely agree that ...*
- *should be on our list*
- *I also think we should ...*
- *And how about visiting ...?*
- *Believe me, they're amazing!*
- *As for a place to stay, ...*
- *What do you think?*
- *I'm looking forward to ...*
- *All the best,*

Sample 5

- *Dear Mrs Smith,*
- *Thank you for your response about ...*
- *I'm available on ...*
- *Regarding the types of films I enjoy, ...*
- *thrillers*
- *... I would love to watch ...*
- *Do you think ... ?*
- *Sincerely,*

Useful Phrases for Emails

More useful phrases

Greetings

- *Hi John,*
- *Hello John,*
- *Dear John,*

Introductory paragraph

- *It's nice / great / good to hear from you.*
- *It's nice / great / good to read your letter.*
- *Thanks a lot for writing!*
- *It was good to receive your letter.*
- *Thank you very much for your letter.*
- *Hope you are doing well.*
- *How's it going?*
- *How are you (doing)?*
- *How are things (going)?*

Reacting to good news

- *I'm (so) glad to hear … (your news).*
- *I'm excited about … (your news.)*
- *It's great to hear/read that …*
- *That's fantastic!*
- *I'm so happy that …*

Reacting to bad news

- *I'm (so) sorry to hear that …*
- *I'm really sorry to read your news.*
- *Sorry to read about*

Introducing paragraphs & ideas

- *As for …,*
- *As to …,*
- *Regarding …,*
- *By the way, …*
- *Hey, did you hear about…?*
- *One more thing, …*

Ending the informal email or letter

- *Well, it's time to say goodbye.*
- *Anyway, I have to go now.*
- *Well, it's time to go.*
- *Anyway, gotta go.*
- *I really hope to hear from you soon.*
- *I'm looking forward to hearing from you.*
- *I hope you write back soon.*
- *Make sure you write back soon.*

Closing formulas

- *Best wishes,*
- *Best,*
- *Sincerely,*
- *Take care,*
- *All my love,*
- *Love,*
- *Lots of love,*
- *See you soon,*
- *Regards,*

Articles

Writing Part 2: Articles

Purpose of an article

The goal of an article is usually to talk about a topic you like or in which you are an expert. Also, your article should aim to keep the reader engaged and, in some cases, recommend whatever it is you are talking about.

Register

Articles are usually expected to be written in standard English with some informal language. Because they are intended to entertain, you can use more relaxed language, using contractions, phrasal verbs and more informal words. Also, it is common to use rhetorical questions and exclamation marks to keep the reader engaged or to make a point. You should address the reader directly and you can use humour where you think it's appropriate.

Structure

Articles usually have a title. If possible, this title should be catchy so it grabs the reader's attention. Then, you should have a paragraph for each aspect you are writing about. In your conclusion, you might be expected to make a recommendation. It is sometimes a good idea to finish your article with a rhetorical question or imperative sentence which asks the reader to take action, especially if you are writing an article for a website.

Giving your opinion

An article is all about your opinion, so feel free to give it wherever you feel it's necessary. Usually, you are asked to write articles about topics you like or are familiar with, so it makes more sense for your opinions to be generally positive. An article is a very personal piece of writing, so you can use first-person sentences freely.

Common topics

You may be asked to write articles on a variety of topics: the Internet, health and fitness, music, plays, hobbies, etc.

How to Write an Article for B1 Preliminary

In this part of the test, you are given a set of instructions to write an article in about 100 words.

Here's an example:

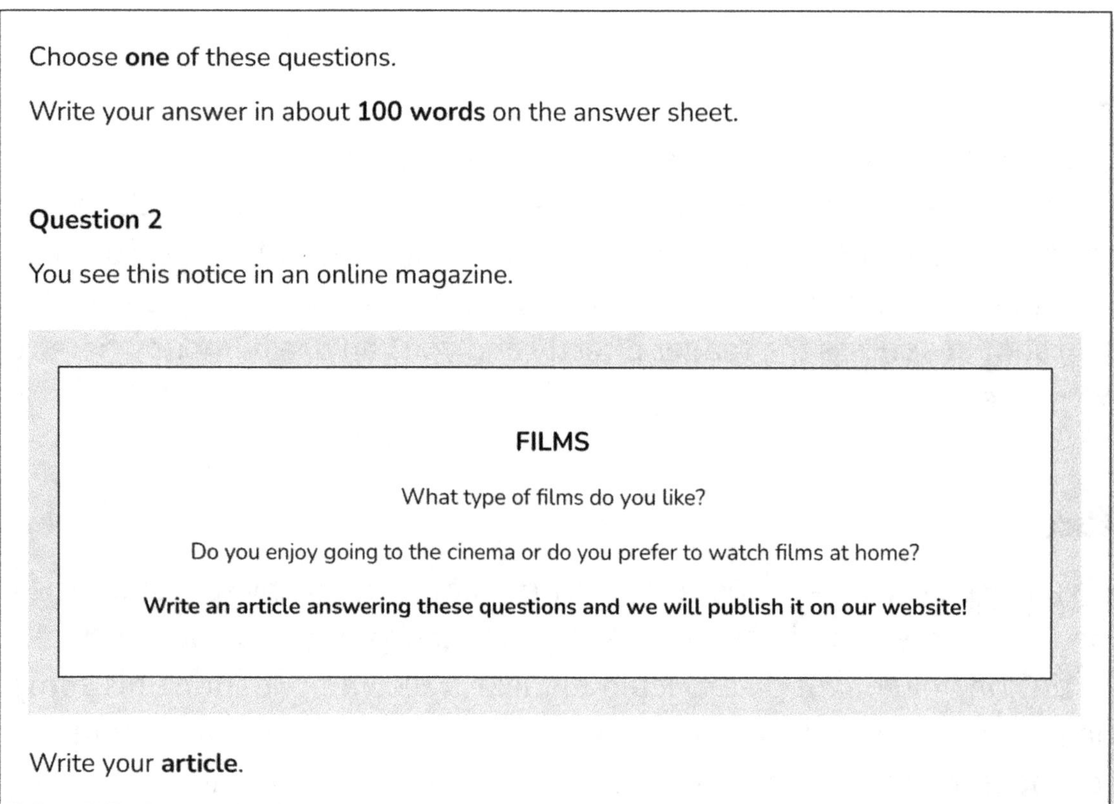

For this particular task, you have to write an article about the type of films you like to watch, also talking about whether you like to watch them at home or at the cinema. As you can see, this is not a very complex topic.

Article Structure

If there is one thing that is important in any piece of writing, regardless of the level, it is that its structure is well defined semantically, grammatically and visually. This is essential.

How to Write an Article for B1 Preliminary (cont.)

In general, an article should always have the following parts:

- Title
- Introduction
- Development of idea 1
- Development of idea 2 (if any)
- Development of idea 3 (if any)
- Conclusion/Recommendation/Call to action

In fact, this kind of structure is repeated in many types of Writings at higher levels, with some slight changes. Now, let's take a look at the following article, where we can see a sample answer to the task on the previous page:

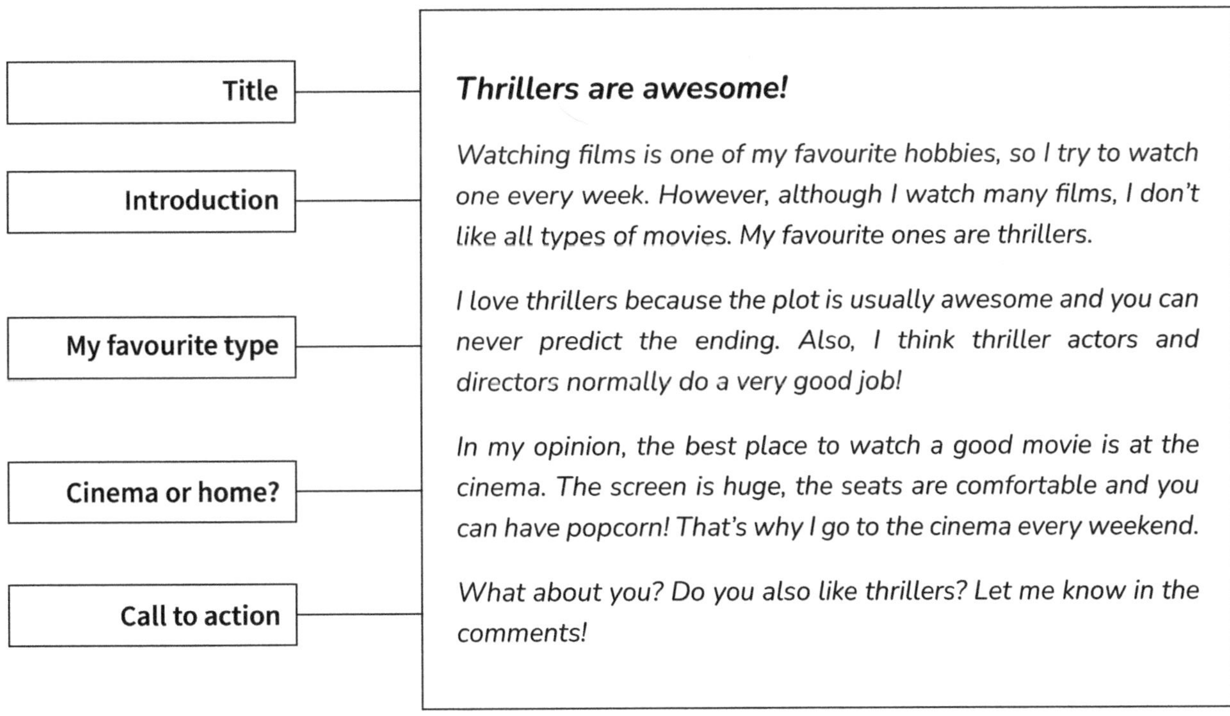

In this example, you can clearly see how the article is divided. While this is a good way to develop and structure the article, it is not necessarily the only correct way to do it. Far from it. Also, notice how the conclusion is simply a series of questions in one line and a call to action (i.e.: *Let me know in the comments!*). Although this seems unusual, the text is supposed to be published on a website, like a blog post. As you know, blogs usually have a comments section, so it might be appropriate to ask the reader to leave a comment about your work. This makes it more natural, authentic and engaging.

Sample Article 1

Instructions

Choose **one** of these questions.

Write your answer in about **100 words** on the answer sheet.

Question 2

You see this notice in an English-language magazine.

RESTAURANT ARTICLES WANTED

Do you eat out often? Why do you like it?

What kind of restaurant do you enjoy? Is there one you would recommend in your town?

Write an article answering these questions and we will publish it on our blog!

Write your **article**.

Do you need someone to mark your article for B1?

Check out KSE Academy's writing assessment service. Scan the QR code on the left with your phone or visit *https://kdp.kseacademy.com/writing-b1-book* for more information. Use the coupon *AMZWB1* for a great discount as a thank you for purchasing this book.

Sample Article 1

Answer

Don't you enjoy eating out?

Do you ever get tired of laying the table? I do! Do you enjoy washing the dishes? I really don't! That's why I believe eating out is great.

I know that eating out is expensive, but I do it a couple of times a week. Instead of spending money in nightclubs or on clothes, I'd rather spend money in a good restaurant, because the food is nice and it's very convenient.

My favourite restaurants are usually Italian (I love pasta!), but my favourite restaurant in my city is a Japanese place called "Kirin". They serve the best sushi!

If you're ever in my city, I recommend that you go to Kirin or any of the Italian restaurants in the centre. You won't regret it!

Sample Article 2

Instructions

Choose **one** of these questions.

Write your answer in about **100 words** on the answer sheet.

Question 2

You see this notice in an English-language magazine.

ARTICLES WANTED FOR OUR LOCAL MAGAZINE

Do you enjoy outdoor activities like hiking? Why do you like hiking? Where do you do it?

Is there a particular place to do outdoor activities that you would recommend to others?
What's so good about it?

Write an article answering these questions and you might get published!

Write your **article**.

Do you need someone to mark your article for B1?

Check out KSE Academy's writing assessment service. Scan the QR code on the left with your phone or visit *https://kdp.kseacademy.com/writing-b1-book* for more information. Use the coupon *AMZWB1* for a great discount as a thank you for purchasing this book.

Sample Article 2

Answer

Outdoor activities and places!

Are you tired of the city? Me too! That's why I like hiking, because I love the feeling of fresh air on my face while I am walking.

One of my favourite areas for trekking is a local mountain nearby. The views from the top are fantastic and hiking up there is always fun!

And if you're looking for the perfect place to do any outdoor activity, I highly recommend the Valley Gardens. There are many spaces prepared for training and it's a silent place, so you can really concentrate.

In short, outdoor activities like hiking are wonderful to take a break and recharge your batteries. And there are some great places around here too!

Sample Article 3

Instructions

Choose **one** of these questions.

Write your answer in about **100 words** on the answer sheet.

Question 2

You see this notice on an English-language blog.

MUSIC BLOG POST

Are you passionate about music? What is your favorite genre and why?

Do you have a favorite musician or band? Why do you enjoy their music?

Write a blog post four our readers and we will publish it online!

Write your **article**.

Do you need someone to mark your article for B1?

Check out KSE Academy's writing assessment service. Scan the QR code on the left with your phone or visit *https://kdp.kseacademy.com/writing-b1-book* for more information. Use the coupon *AMZWB1* for a great discount as a thank you for purchasing this book.

Sample Article 3

Answer

Music and me!

If you're like me, you're always looking for new bands and genres to listen to. Because music is great, isn't it? Listening to music is my favourite hobby of all time!

My favorite genre is definitely rock. I love the energy and emotion of rock songs. Every morning, I press play and listen to a few rock tunes while I have breakfast.

In my opinion, the best musician ever is Bruce Springsteen. I have always admired his lyrics, and I think his concerts are really amazing. He's the best!

How about you? What's your favourite musician? Do you also enjoy rock, like me? Tell me about it in the comments!

Sample Article 4

Instructions

Choose **one** of these questions.

Write your answer in about **100 words** on the answer sheet.

Question 2

You see this notice on an English-language website.

FRIENDSHIP ARTICLES

Is friendship important to you? Why or why not?

Who is your closest friend and why? How did you meet?
Do you see each other often?

Write an article and we will publish it for our online readers.

Write your **article**.

Do you need someone to mark your article for B1?

Check out KSE Academy's writing assessment service. Scan the QR code on the left with your phone or visit *https://kdp.kseacademy.com/writing-b1-book* for more information. Use the coupon *AMZWB1* for a great discount as a thank you for purchasing this book.

Sample Article 4

Answer

The importance of friends

Friendships are extremely important for everyone and spending time socialising with other people is essential. Don't you agree?

In my case, being with my friends makes me really happy. When we meet up, we do many things together and we help each other all the time.

My closest friend is called Loraine. We met in high school many years ago and we're still in touch. We both loved the same music and we became best friends instantly. I love her so much!

To sum up, having friends is really important if you want to be happy. And if you have a friend like Loraine, even better!

Sample Article 5

Instructions

Choose **one** of these questions.

Write your answer in about **100 words** on the answer sheet.

Question 2

You see this notice on the website of an English-language local guidebook of your town.

> ### SHOPPING IN TOWN
>
> What's a great place in town to go shopping and why?
>
> Do you enjoy going shopping?
>
> When was the last time you went shopping around here?
>
> **Write an article for the local guidebook.**

Write your **article**.

Do you need someone to mark your article for B1?

Check out KSE Academy's writing assessment service. Scan the QR code on the left with your phone or visit *https://kdp.kseacademy.com/writing-b1-book* for more information. Use the coupon *AMZWB1* for a great discount as a thank you for purchasing this book.

Sample Article 5

Answer

The best mall!

If you're looking for a great place to go shopping in town, I highly recommend the local mall. It has many fashion stores, tech shops and a few nice restaurants.

Personally, I really enjoy going shopping there, especially when I need clothes. If have some money and free time, I usually spend the afternoon at the mall. It's a lot of fun!

The last time I went shopping was last weekend. I needed a new pair of trainers, so I decided to visit the mall and I found a great bargain!

Overall, the mall is definitely the best place to go shopping in town. If you're around here and have some time to kill, you should visit it!

Useful Phrases for Articles

Sample 1

- *Do you ever … ?*
- *I do!*
- *I really don't!*
- *That's why …*
- *Instead of …,*
- *I'd rather …*
- *convenient*
- *My favourite …*
- *If you're ever in my city, I recommend that …*
- *You won't regret it!*

Sample 2

- *Are you tired of … ? Me too!*
- *I love the feeling of … while I am …*
- *One of my favourite …*
- *trekking*
- *nearby*
- *The views …*
- *… hiking up there is always fun!*
- *And if you're looking …,*
- *I highly recommend …*
- *In short, …*
- *outdoor activities*
- *… are wonderful to take a break …*
- *recharge your batteries*

Sample 3

- *If you're like me, …*
- *… new bands and genres to listen to.*
- *… my favourite hobby of all time!*
- *… is definitely rock.*
- *… listen to a few rock tunes while …*
- *In my opinion, …*
- *the best musician ever*
- *I have always admired his lyrics, …*

- *How about you?*
- *Do you also … ?*
- *Tell me about it in the comments!*

Sample 4

- *… extremely important for …*
- *… is essential.*
- *Don't you agree?*
- *In my case, …*
- *When we meet up, …*
- *… we help each other …*
- *My closest friend …*
- *… we're still in touch.*
- *we became best friends …*
- *To sum up, …*
- *…, even better!*

Sample 5

- *I highly recommend …*
- *Personally, …*
- *I really enjoy …*
- *I usually spend …*
- *It's a lot of fun!*
- *…, so I decided to …*
- *I found a great bargain!*
- *Overall, …*
- *If you're around here …,*
- *… have some time to kill, …*

Useful Phrases for Articles

More useful phrases
Opening paragraph

- *Have you ever … ?*
- *Do you ever wonder … ?*
- *What do you think about … ?*
- *Are you one of those people who … ?*
- *If you're like me, …*

Introducing ideas

- *First, …*
- *In the first place, …*
- *Second, …*
- *Finally, …*
- *As for, …*
- *In addition, …*
- *Moreover, …*
- *However, …*

Engaging the reader

- *Don't worry!*
- *Keep on reading!*
- *Imagine that…*
- *What about you?*
- *Isn't that great?*
- *Let me know in the comments!*
- *Even better!*

Conclusion paragraph

- *In conclusion, …*
- *To sum up, …*
- *On the whole, …*
- *Overall, …*
- *In short, …*

Stories

Writing Part 2: Stories

Purpose of a story

A story is simply an account of events of imaginary or real people told for entertainment. Therefore, the purpose of every story is to entertain the reader. Precisely for this reason, you have more freedom in your writing, as you can make everything up. But just like any other type of text, a story must follow a structure that makes sense to the reader.

Register

A story at B1 level is expected to be written in standard English with some informal language if it fits the context. Because they are intended to entertain, you can use more relaxed language, using contractions, phrasal verbs and more informal words. Also, it is common to use direct speech (when the characters in the story speak or think) and exclamation marks to express strong feelings and keep the reader engaged. Furthermore, when writing your story, you should pay close attention to any names or pronouns used in the opening sentence. Then, ensure your story follows the same pattern. For example, if the story begins in the third person, it should probably continue that way.

Structure

Generally, a text telling a story can be divided into these parts: title, exposition, action and resolution. The title must be related to the main theme of the story without giving away any spoilers; the exposition is the beginning of the story, where the characters and the location of the action are introduced; the action is where the main events of the story take place; and the resolution is where the action is resolved and the story concludes, usually without loose ends.

Common topics

The topic of the story will depend entirely on the first sentence, which is given in the instructions. There is no set list of possible topics for stories, but the first sentence is always expected to be in the past, which determines the whole timeline of your story.

How to Write a Story for B1 Preliminary

According to the Longman Dictionary, a story is "a description of how something happened, that is intended to entertain people, and may be true or imaginary". For this reason, precisely, you have plenty more freedom to write, as you can make up most of the story. But just like it happens with every other type of writing, a story must follow a particular structure which makes sense to the reader. So let's move on to the different parts of a story.

Parts of a story

A story can roughly be divided into the following parts:

- **Title**: The title should either summarise the story (without spoilers) or have something to do with the main theme.

- **Exposition**: This is the beginning of the story, where the characters and setting are established. It serves as the introduction to the next part, the action, and the so-called conflict of our story.

- **Action**: In this part, the characters deal with conflict and do something to solve it.

- **Resolution**: This is where the conflict is resolved and the story concludes with an ending, normally without any loose ends.

Now that we know the different parts of a story, let's take a look at the following sample instructions of a B1 Preliminary Writing Part 2 task, for question 3:

Choose **one** of these questions.

Write your answer in about **100 words** on the answer sheet.

Question 3

Your English teacher has asked you to write a story.

Your story must begin with this sentence:

I felt nervous when the phone rang.

Write your **story**.

How to Write a Story for B1 Preliminary (cont.)

And here's a sample answer to the task on the previous page:

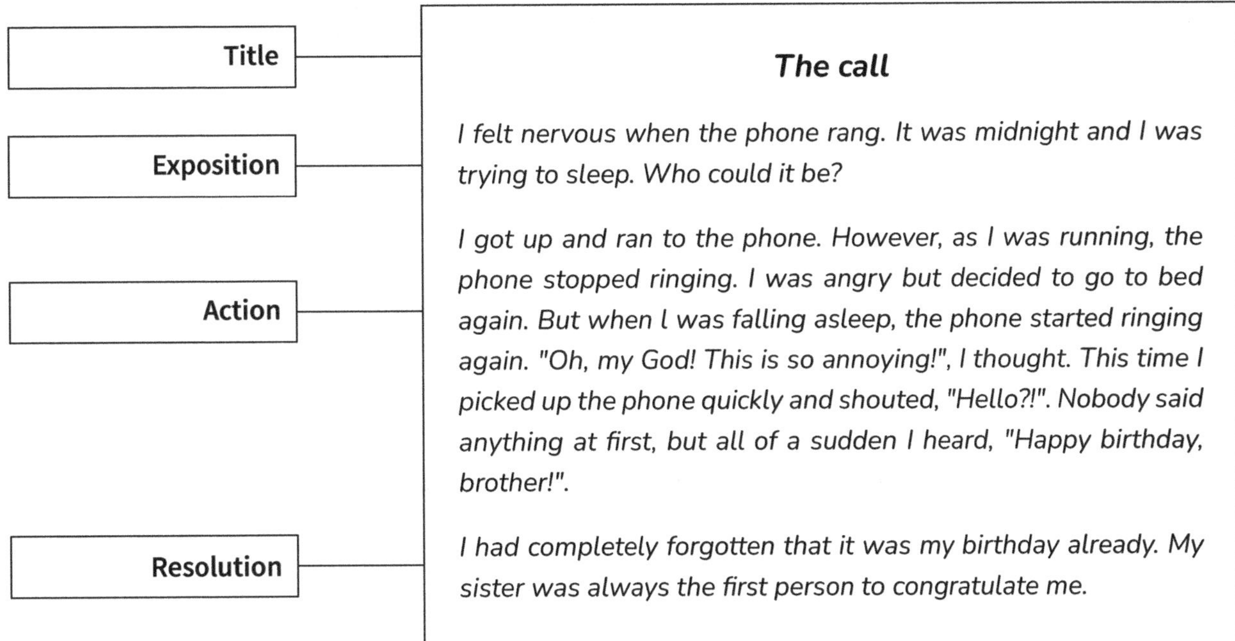

In the example above you can see the different parts of a story very well defined. Firstly, there's the **title** (i.e.: *The call*), which is on the first line the reader can see. In your exam, you won't be able to use bold lettering, so you can use CAPITALS instead.

Then comes the **exposition**, which <u>must start with the sentence given in the instructions</u>. Notice how the first sentence is defining that the story should be narrated in the first person.

Later, in the **action**, you can see how the main character is facing a conflict or problem (i.e.: The phone is ringing late at night and they don't know who is calling).

In the last paragraph comes the **resolution**, in which the character finds the answer or solution to the issue (i.e.: It's the main character's birthday and the person calling is their sister, to congratulate them).

Something you must pay attention to the story above is the range of past tenses used. We can see past simple forms (*it was, I got up*, etc.), past continuous forms (*I was trying to sleep, I was running*, etc.) and past perfect forms (*I had completely forgotten*). Also, there is direct speech with correct punctuation (E.g.: *"Oh, my God! This is so annoying!"*)

Finally, notice how your story should be visually appealing and easy to read. For this reason, I recommend writing clearly (if you do the paper-based exam) and leaving an empty line between paragraphs.

Sample Story 1

Instructions

Choose **one** of these questions.

Write your answer in about **100 words** on the answer sheet.

Question 3

Your English teacher has asked you to write a story.

Your story must begin with this sentence:

John felt angry as he got off the train.

Write your **story**.

Do you need someone to mark your story for B1?

Check out KSE Academy's writing assessment service. Scan the QR code on the left with your phone or visit *https://kdp.kseacademy.com/writing-b1-book* for more information. Use the coupon *AMZWB1* for a great discount as a thank you for purchasing this book.

Sample Story 1

Answer

The broken train

John felt angry as he got off the train. The train had broken down and they had stopped in the middle of the countryside.

Everyone was getting off the train, speaking to each other. But John was tired and he didn't want to talk much. So he sat under a tree and decided to take a nap.

John was sleeping when, without a warning, he heard the sound of a train moving. All of a sudden, he woke up and saw the train moving away. He shouted, "Stop the train, please!", but nobody heard him. Although he ran and ran, John couldn't reach the train.

In the end, he gave up running and called his parents, who picked him up a few hours later.

Sample Story 2

Instructions

Choose **one** of these questions.

Write your answer in about **100 words** on the answer sheet.

Question 3

Your English teacher has asked you to write a story.

Your story must begin with this sentence:

> Robert was excited about the box he had received.

Write your **story**.

Do you need someone to mark your story for B1?

Check out KSE Academy's writing assessment service. Scan the QR code on the left with your phone or visit *https://kdp.kseacademy.com/writing-b1-book* for more information. Use the coupon *AMZWB1* for a great discount as a thank you for purchasing this book.

Sample Story 2

Answer

What's in the box?

Robert was excited about the box he had received. It had been sent to him and he had no idea what was inside. The box had a rectangular shape and it was quite large.

As he took off the wrapping paper, he was feeling nervous. "What's inside?" he thought. Right away, he knew what it was. Inside the box, there was a brand new guitar, exactly what he wanted for his birthday. He couldn't believe it!

Robert spent the rest of the day practising and learning to play new songs. He was thrilled to have such a special gift. He couldn't wait to show it to his friends!

Sample Story 3

Instructions

Choose **one** of these questions.

Write your answer in about **100 words** on the answer sheet.

Question 3

Your English teacher has asked you to write a story.

Your story must begin with this sentence:

Joanne paused the music and took her headphones off.

Write your **story**.

Do you need someone to mark your story for B1?

Check out KSE Academy's writing assessment service. Scan the QR code on the left with your phone or visit *https://kdp.kseacademy.com/writing-b1-book* for more information. Use the coupon *AMZWB1* for a great discount as a thank you for purchasing this book.

Sample Story 3

Answer

A new best friend

Joanne paused the music and took her headphones off. She had already studied enough and needed a break. She stood up and decided to go for a walk in the park.

As she walked through the park, she saw a group of kids playing soccer. Joanne had always enjoyed playing sports, so she asked them, "Can I join you?" The kids passed her the ball and they all played together for a bit.

After the game, Joanne saw a dog following her. "Are you lost?", asked Joanne. The dog just looked at her. There was nobody around, so Joanne decided to take it home. "I think I just found my new best friend!" she thought.

Sample Story 4

Instructions

Choose **one** of these questions.

Write your answer in about **100 words** on the answer sheet.

Question 3

Your English teacher has asked you to write a story.

Your story must begin with this sentence:

Ben hadn't seen his brother for five years.

Write your **story**.

Do you need someone to mark your story for B1?

Check out KSE Academy's writing assessment service. Scan the QR code on the left with your phone or visit *https://kdp.kseacademy.com/writing-b1-book* for more information. Use the coupon *AMZWB1* for a great discount as a thank you for purchasing this book.

Sample Story 4

Answer

An unexpected visit

Ben hadn't seen his brother for five years. They were good friends when they were kids, but then they lost contact. Now, five years later, they were going to meet up again.

His brother, Jack, had called him the day before because he wanted to visit him. Ben was excited but also a bit nervous. "What does he want?", Ben was thinking while he was waiting for Jack to arrive. Suddenly, the doorbell rang, so Ben got up and opened the door.

Jack was standing outside, but he hadn't come alone. Next to him, there was a woman and a girl. "Hello, Ben," said Jack. "I'd like you to meet my wife and your niece". Ben smiled and hugged his brother.

Sample Story 5

Instructions

Choose **one** of these questions.

Write your answer in about **100 words** on the answer sheet.

Question 3

Your English teacher has asked you to write a story.

Your story must begin with this sentence:

Someone called my name as I entered the waiting room.

Write your **story**.

Do you need someone to mark your story for B1?

Check out KSE Academy's writing assessment service. Scan the QR code on the left with your phone or visit *https://kdp.kseacademy.com/writing-b1-book* for more information. Use the coupon *AMZWB1* for a great discount as a thank you for purchasing this book.

Sample Story 5

Answer

At the doctor's

Someone called my name as I entered the waiting room. I turned around and saw my friend Rachel.

"Hey, what are you doing here?" I asked her. "I'm here to see the doctor because I don't feel well," she replied. I didn't feel very well either.

We both sat down and started talking. Suddenly, the nurse called Rachel, so she stood up and left.

After some time, Rachel came out and she looked happy. "The doctor said I just have a cold. Nothing serious," Rachel told me. I was very happy for her. "I hope I just have a cold, too," I told her.

Finally, we said goodbye and I said I would call her at the weekend. Seeing Rachel had made me happy.

Useful Phrases for Stories

Sample 1

- *The train had broken down …*
- *Everyone was getting off the train …*
- *… and decided to take a nap.*
- *…, without a warning, …*
- *All of a sudden, …*
- *He shouted, "Stop the train, please!"*
- *Although he ran …,*
- *In the end, …*

Sample 2

- *It had been sent to him …*
- *… he had no idea what was inside.*
- *a rectangular shape*
- *quite large*
- *As he took off the wrapping paper, …*
- *Right away, …*
- *a brand new guitar*
- *He couldn't believe it!*
- *the rest of the day*
- *He was thrilled …*
- *such a special gift*
- *He wouldn't wait to …*

Sample 3

- *She had already studied enough …*
- *… needed a break.*
- *She stood up and decided to …*
- *… go for a walk in the park.*
- *As she walked through the park …*
- *… they all played together for a bit.*
- *After the game …,*
- *There was nobody around, so …*

Sample 4

- *…, but they had lost contact.*
- *Now, five years later, …*
- *… to meet up again.*
- *His brother, Jack, had called …*
- *… excited but also a bit nervous.*
- *… Ben was thinking while he was waiting …*
- *Suddenly, the doorbell rang, …*
- *Jack was standing outside, …*
- *"I'd like you to meet … "*
- *… your niece.*
- *… hugged his brother.*

Sample 5

- *I turned around and saw …*
- *"Hey, what are you doing here?"*
- *"… I don't feel well,"*
- *I didn't feel very well either.*
- *… she stood up and left.*
- *After some time, …*
- *… she looked happy.*
- *"… . Nothing serious,"*
- *"I hope I just … "*
- *Finally, we said goodbye and …*
- *… I said I would call her at the weekend.*

Useful Phrases for Stories

More useful phrases
Beginning a story

- *It all began …*
- *When I first …*
- *At the beginning …*
- *It was a hot summer/cold winter day.*

Time expressions

- *Then, …*
- *After that, …*
- *Not long afterwards, …*
- *As soon as …,*
- *While …,*
- *Meanwhile, …*
- *As …,*
- *Some time later, …*
- *A little later, …*
- *… minutes later, …*
- *a moment later, …*
- *Later (that morning/afternoon/day/night), …*
- *Just then, …*

Creating suspense

- *Suddenly, …*
- *All of a sudden, …*
- *Without warning, …*
- *Just at that moment, …*
- *Unexpectedly, …*
- *Out of the blue, …*
- *Out of nowhere, …*
- *(…) Right away, …*
- *(…) Straight away, …*

Direct speech

- *"I'm coming with you," she said.*
- *She said, "I'm coming with you."*
- *"Do you like it?" he asked.*
- *"Don't do it!" he screamed.*

Concluding a story

- *In the end, …*
- *Finally, …*
- *When it was all over, …*
- *Eventually, …*
- *After everything that (had) happened, …*
- *Luckily, …*

Verb tenses

- **Past simple and continuous:**
    - *It was midnight and I was trying to sleep.*

- **Past perfect and simple:**
    - *I had completely forgotten it was my birthday.*

- **Past simple:**
    - *This time I picked up the phone quickly and shouted, «Hello?!».*

Essential Connectors for B1 Writing

Introduction

Two of the most important features of any good piece of writing are **coherence** and **cohesion**. In order to have a coherent text, we must ensure that our ideas are well organised and that they follow a logical progression from beginning to end.

To have adequate coherence and cohesion in a text, apart from a proper use of syntactical elements, we must make good use of English connectors. These connectors are one of the elements that B1 students find most difficult to start incorporating into their writing. For this reason, in this section, we are going to learn to use a range of B1 connectors in English.

What are English connectors?

Linguistic connectors, also known as discourse markers or linking words, are **words or phrases that connect different parts of a text**. They help to create coherence and cohesion by signalling the relationships between ideas and indicating how they are related to each other. Some examples of linguistic connectors include *and, or, because, although, so, in addition*, etc.

In this section, we will categorise them into three groups: **reason, purpose and result**; **contrast**; and **addition**.

Reason, purpose and result connectors

because (of), as, since

We use these three linking words to give a reason for something. "Because" is more common than "as" and "since".

> *She didn't tell him <u>because/as/since</u> she was afraid to.*

We use "because of" when the reason is a noun, not a sentence.

> *Jack knew Laura <u>because of</u> his brother.*

> *We didn't recognise him <u>because of</u> the sunglasses.*

So & therefore

We use "so" and "therefore" when we want to express the result of something. "So" usually appears in the middle of a sentence, whereas "therefore" sounds more formal and it normally comes at the beginning of the sentence and is followed by a comma.

I'm really tired <u>so</u> I won't go out tonight.

I'm really tired. <u>Therefore,</u> I won't go out tonight.

To & In order to

We use "to" and "in order" to when we explain why we do something, the reason or purpose. They are always followed by an infinitive.

I have joined an academy <u>to</u> learn English.

I've joined an academy <u>in order to</u> learn English.

We can also answer a *Why…?* question using "to" or "in order to".

A: *Why have you joined an academy?*

B: <u>*To/In order to*</u> *learn English.*

Contrast connectors

But, although & though

These linking words connect two contrasting ideas and are followed by a clause (pronoun/noun + verb). "But" normally appears in the middle of a sentence, preceded by a comma, while "although/though" can go in the middle or at the beginning.

The hotel was excellent, <u>but</u> the food was not good.

The hotel was excellent <u>although/though</u> the food was not good.

<u>*Although/though*</u> *the food was not good, the hotel was excellent.*

Essential Connectors for B1 Writing (cont.)

In spite of & despite

"In spite of" and "despite" are used to express a contrast between two ideas. These connectors are followed by a noun or an *-ing* phrase, and never by a clause (pronoun/ noun + verb). They can be used either at the beginning or in the middle of a sentence.

The hotel was excellent <u>despite</u> the food being bad/the bad food.

The hotel was excellent <u>in spite of</u> the food being bad/the bad food.

<u>Despite</u> the food being bad/the bad food, the hotel was excellent.

<u>In spite of</u> the food being bad/the bad food, the hotel was excellent.

However

"However" is a word which connects two different contrasting sentences. It's normally used at the beginning of a sentence and should be followed by a comma.

The hotel was excellent. <u>However,</u> the food was awful.

Some people tend to put on weight. <u>However,</u> it's never inevitable.

Addition connectors

Also, too, in addition, moreover

We use these linking words to add more information to something we have said.

"Too" normally goes at the end and is used in positive sentences. "Also" (as a sentence adverb), "in addition" and "moreover" usually go at the beginning.

Buying a car is a long-term commitment. <u>Also,</u> a car is very expensive to run.

Buying a car is a long-term commitment. <u>In addition,</u> a car is very expensive to run.

Buying a car is a long-term commitment. <u>Moreover,</u> a car is very expensive to run.

Buying a car is a long-term commitment. A car is very expensive to run, <u>too</u>.

All these words will definitely be essential in your writings for B1 Preliminary (PET) or even B2 First (FCE), so make sure you know how to use them properly.

67

Writing Assessment

Who assesses candidates' writing tasks?

Cambridge Assessment English has a team of trained examiners who mark the writing scripts in a secure online marking environment. These examiners must prove, every year, that they are competent to assess. This is done through an internal certification and monitoring process.

What is assessed?

Writing examiners award marks to each writing task using a Writing Assessment Scale. This scale has been developed to reflect the criteria set by the Common European Framework of Reference for Languages (CEFR). In accordance with the CEFR, the Writing Assessment Scale is divided into four categories:

Content

This focuses on whether candidates have fulfilled the task, that is, if they have really done what they were asked to do.

Communicative achievement

This refers to how appropriate the writing is for the task, focusing on the usage of the appropriate register.

Organisation

This section focuses on how candidates organise their writing, on its progression and whether it is logical and ordered.

Language

This focuses on grammar and vocabulary, as well as the range of language and the accuracy of the piece of writing.

How is writing assessed?

In order to assess a piece of writing for B1 Preliminary, the previously described subscale categories are divided into six so-called bands, which range from 0 to 5. Each band represents a level of performance.

The following points must be taken into account in order to understand how to mark Cambridge writing tasks:

- **Band 0** is the **lowest possible mark**, and 5 is the highest.

- **Band 3** is considered the **lowest mark to pass**.

- Anything **below Band 3 is not considered B1** performance.

- Only **full marks are awarded**, no half marks.

The maximum score candidates can get is 40 (5 marks per category; 20 marks per task). The minimum score to pass the whole Writing paper is 24 marks.

In the following section, there is a writing mark sheet which can be used to assess B1 writing tasks.

Do you need someone to mark your writing tasks?

Check out KSE Academy's writing assessment service. Scan the QR code on the left with your phone or visit *https://kdp.kseacademy.com/writing-b1-book* for more information. Use the coupon *AMZWB1* for a great discount as a thank you for purchasing this book.

Writing Mark Sheet

Candidate _______________________________   **Date**

dd	mm	yyyy

Writing Part 1

Content	0	1	2	3	4	5
Communicative achievement	0	1	2	3	4	5
Organisation	0	1	2	3	4	5
Language	0	1	2	3	4	5
TOTAL MARKS	____ / 20					

Writing Part 2

Content	0	1	2	3	4	5
Communicative achievement	0	1	2	3	4	5
Organisation	0	1	2	3	4	5
Language	0	1	2	3	4	5
TOTAL MARKS	____ / 20					

Band descriptors

Content	• Relevance to the task
	• How well the target reader is informed
Communicative achievement	• Conventions of the communicative task
	• Hold reader's attention
	• Communicativeness
Organisation	• Coherence
	• Cohesive devices
	• Organisational patterns
Language	• Range of vocabulary
	• Grammatical forms
	• Accuracy

Writing Tasks Overview

The following table shows a summary of the features of every writing task type. It is extremely important to be familiar with the basic characteristics of every kind of task, especially to achieve a good mark in the communicative achievement subscale.

	Style	Purpose	Title	Subheadings	Paragraphs	Common topics
Emails	Informal Standard	React Plan Propose Recommend Inform Decide	X	X	3 - 4 + formulas	Email to a friend Letter to a relative Email to a teacher Etc.
Articles	Informal Standard	Inform Entertain Describe Recommend	✓	X	3 - 4	Music Sport Eating out Friends Leisure activities Etc.
Stories	Standard	Inform Propose Decide	✓	X	3 - 4	-

Sample Test 1

PRELIMINARY ENGLISH TEST

Writing

Time 45 minutes

INSTRUCTIONS TO CANDIDATES

Do not open this question paper until you are told to do so.

Write your name, centre number and candidate number on your answer sheet if they are not already there.

Read the instructions for each part of the paper carefully.

Answer the Part 1 question and one question from Part 2.

Write your answers on the answer sheet.

Write clearly in **pen**, not pencil. You may make alterations, but make sure your work is easy to read.

You **must** complete the answer sheet within the time limit.

At the end of the test, hand in both this question paper and your answer sheet.

INFORMATION FOR CANDIDATES

Each question in this paper carries equal marks.

Part 1

You **must** answer this question.

Write your answer in about **100 words** on the answer sheet.

Question 1

Read this email from your English-speaking friend Ruth and the notes you have made.

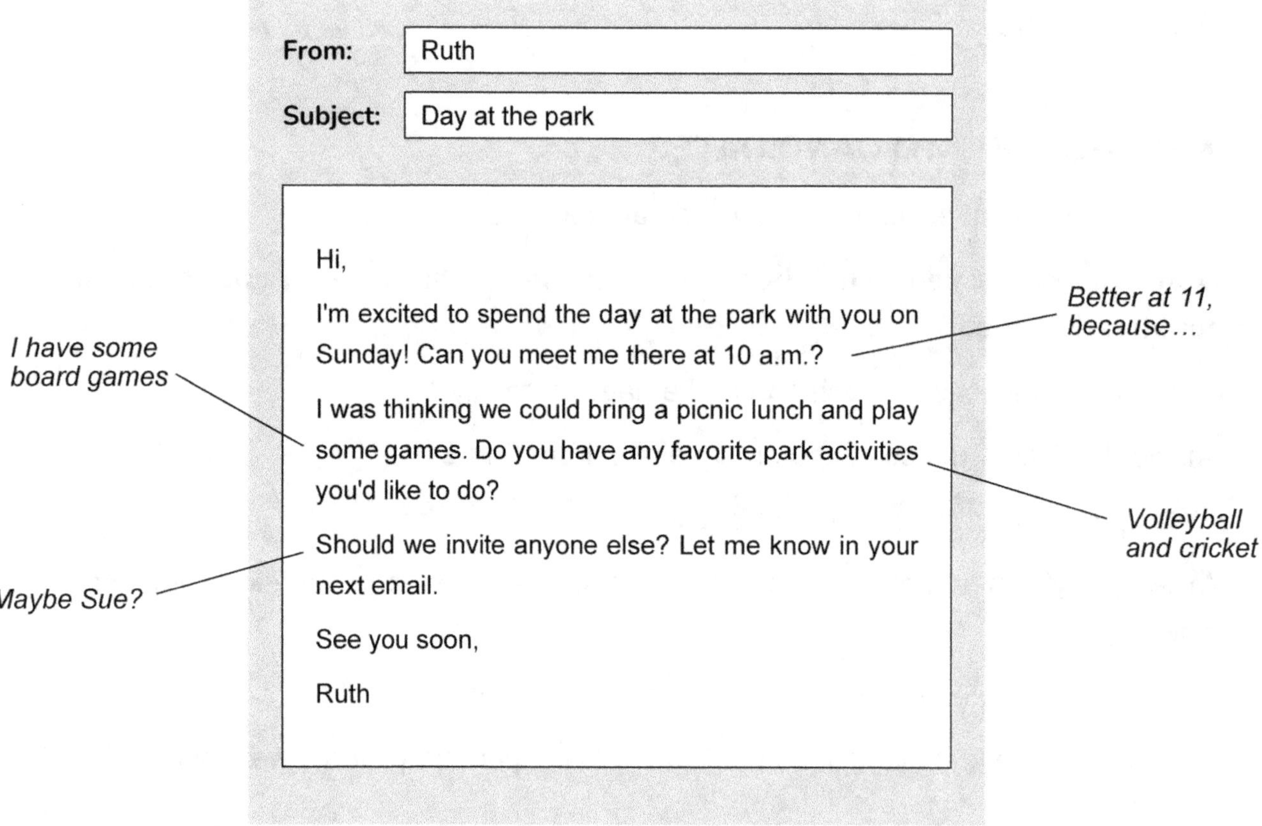

Write your **email** to Ruth using **all the notes**.

Do you need someone to mark your writing tasks?

Check out KSE Academy's writing assessment service. Scan the QR code on the left with your phone or visit *https://kdp.kseacademy.com/writing-b1-book* for more information. Use the coupon *AMZWB1* for a great discount as a thank you for purchasing this book.

Part 2

Choose **one** of these questions.

Write your answer in about **100 words** on the answer sheet.

Question 2

You see this notice on an English-language website about your town.

OUR CRAZY WEATHER

What's your favorite type of weather and why?

What activities do you like to do during different types of weather?

Do you have any tips for visitors?

Write an article for our website. We will publish the best ones!

Write your **article**.

Question 3

Your English teacher has asked you to write a story.

Your story must begin with this sentence:

Samantha heard a noise downstairs.

Write your **story**.

Do you need someone to mark your writing tasks?

Check out KSE Academy's writing assessment service. Scan the QR code on the left with your phone or visit *https://kdp.kseacademy.com/writing-b1-book* for more information. Use the coupon *AMZWB1* for a great discount as a thank you for purchasing this book.

Sample Test 2

PRELIMINARY ENGLISH TEST

Writing

Time 45 minutes

INSTRUCTIONS TO CANDIDATES

Do not open this question paper until you are told to do so.

Write your name, centre number and candidate number on your answer sheet if they are not already there.

Read the instructions for each part of the paper carefully.

Answer the Part 1 question and one question from Part 2.

Write your answers on the answer sheet.

Write clearly in **pen**, not pencil. You may make alterations, but make sure your work is easy to read.

You **must** complete the answer sheet within the time limit.

At the end of the test, hand in both this question paper and your answer sheet.

INFORMATION FOR CANDIDATES

Each question in this paper carries equal marks.

Part 1

You **must** answer this question.

Write your answer in about **100 words** on the answer sheet.

Question 1

Read this email from your English-speaking friend Josh and the notes you have made.

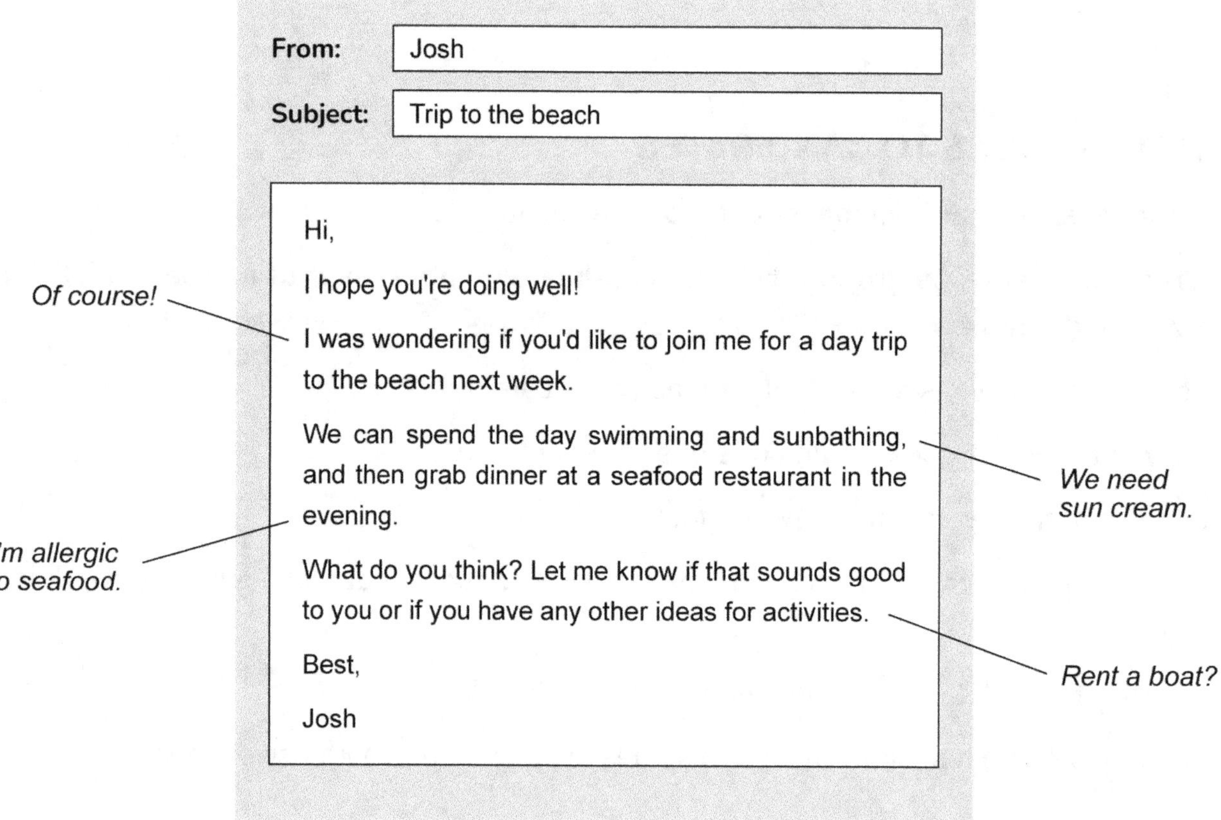

Write your **email** to Josh using **all the notes**.

Do you need someone to mark your writing tasks?

Check out KSE Academy's writing assessment service. Scan the QR code on the left with your phone or visit *https://kdp.kseacademy.com/writing-b1-book* for more information. Use the coupon *AMZWB1* for a great discount as a thank you for purchasing this book.

Part 2

Choose **one** of these questions.

Write your answer in about **100 words** on the answer sheet.

Question 2

You see this notice in an English-language magazine about cooking.

COOKING AT HOME

Do you enjoy cooking at home?

What are some of your favorite dishes to make?

Where do you like to shop for ingredients in town?

Write an article for our readers.

Write your **article**.

Question 3

Your English teacher has asked you to write a story.

Your story must begin with this sentence:

The old man sat quietly on the bench.

Write your **story**.

Do you need someone to mark your writing tasks?

Check out KSE Academy's writing assessment service. Scan the QR code on the left with your phone or visit *https://kdp.kseacademy.com/writing-b1-book* for more information. Use the coupon *AMZWB1* for a great discount as a thank you for purchasing this book.

THIS PAGE IS PHOTOCOPIABLE

Sample
Test 3

PRELIMINARY ENGLISH TEST

Writing

Time   45 minutes

INSTRUCTIONS TO CANDIDATES

Do not open this question paper until you are told to do so.

Write your name, centre number and candidate number on your answer sheet if they are not already there.

Read the instructions for each part of the paper carefully.

Answer the Part 1 question and one question from Part 2.

Write your answers on the answer sheet.

Write clearly in **pen**, not pencil. You may make alterations, but make sure your work is easy to read.

You **must** complete the answer sheet within the time limit.

At the end of the test, hand in both this question paper and your answer sheet.

INFORMATION FOR CANDIDATES

Each question in this paper carries equal marks.

Part 1

You **must** answer this question.

Write your answer in about **100 words** on the answer sheet.

Question 1

Read this email from your English-speaking friend Tom and the notes you have made.

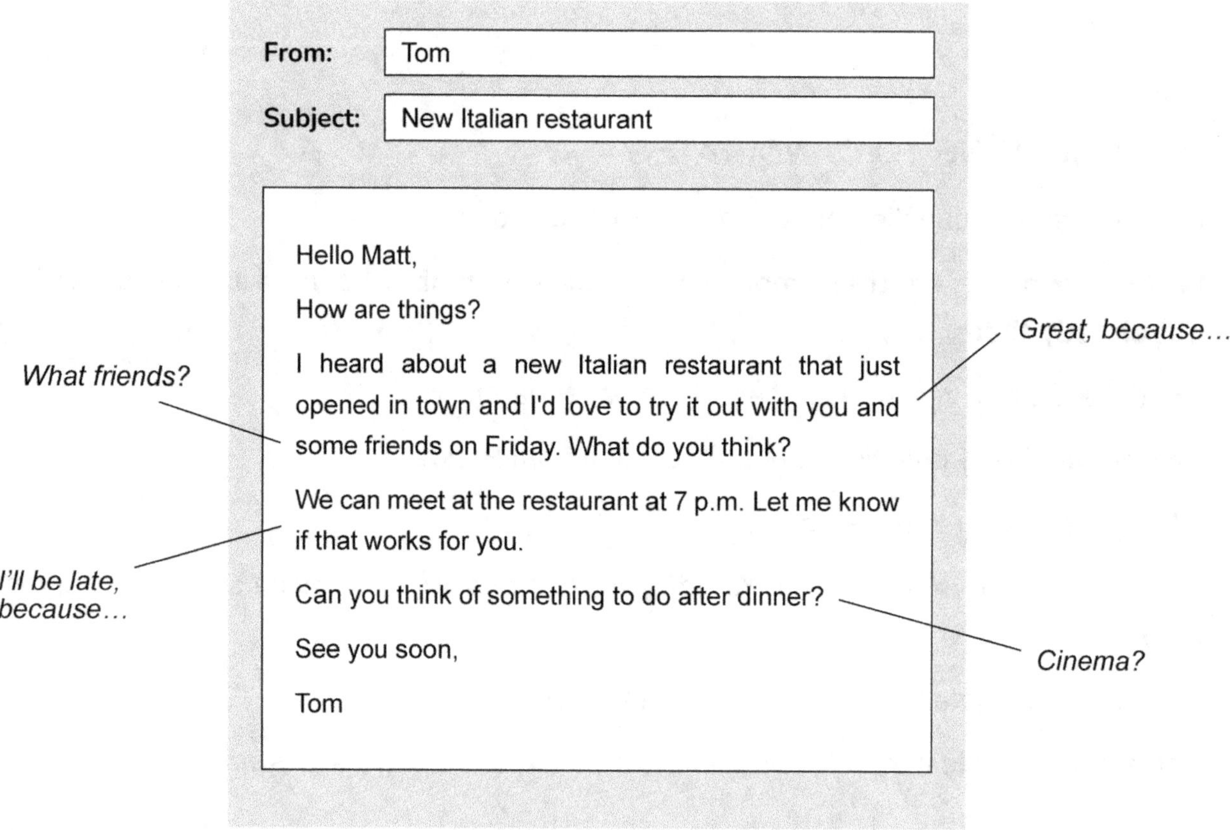

Write your **email** to Tom using **all the notes**.

Do you need someone to mark your writing tasks?

Check out KSE Academy's writing assessment service. Scan the QR code on the left with your phone or visit *https://kdp.kseacademy.com/writing-b1-book* for more information. Use the coupon *AMZWB1* for a great discount as a thank you for purchasing this book.

Part 2

Choose **one** of these questions.

Write your answer in about **100 words** on the answer sheet.

Question 2

You see this notice on an English-language website.

SPENDING TIME AT HOME

Do you enjoy spending time at home?

Do you prefer to spend your time at home alone or with friends?

What are some of your favorite activities to do at home?

Write an article for our website. We will publish the most interesting ones!

Write your **article**.

Question 3

Your English teacher has asked you to write a story.

Your story must begin with this sentence:

Claire was watching TV when someone knocked on her door.

Write your **story**.

Do you need someone to mark your writing tasks?

Check out KSE Academy's writing assessment service. Scan the QR code on the left with your phone or visit *https://kdp.kseacademy.com/writing-b1-book* for more information. Use the coupon *AMZWB1* for a great discount as a thank you for purchasing this book.

Sample
Test 4

PRELIMINARY ENGLISH TEST

Writing

Time   45 minutes

INSTRUCTIONS TO CANDIDATES

Do not open this question paper until you are told to do so.

Write your name, centre number and candidate number on your answer sheet if they are not already there.

Read the instructions for each part of the paper carefully.

Answer the Part 1 question and one question from Part 2.

Write your answers on the answer sheet.

Write clearly in **pen**, not pencil. You may make alterations, but make sure your work is easy to read.

You **must** complete the answer sheet within the time limit.

At the end of the test, hand in both this question paper and your answer sheet.

INFORMATION FOR CANDIDATES

Each question in this paper carries equal marks.

Part 1

You **must** answer this question.

Write your answer in about **100 words** on the answer sheet.

Question 1

Read this email from your English-speaking friend Sean and the notes you have made.

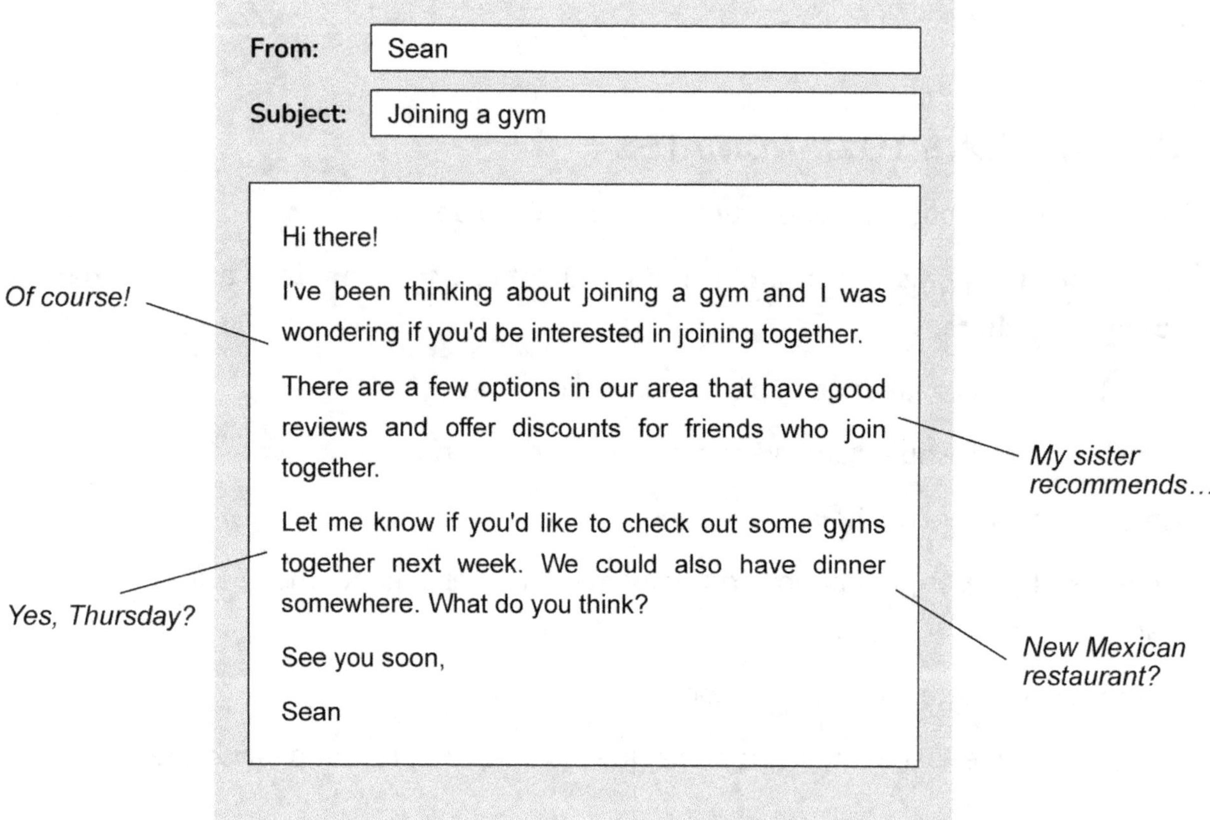

Write your **email** to Sean using **all the notes**.

Do you need someone to mark your writing tasks?

Check out KSE Academy's writing assessment service. Scan the QR code on the left with your phone or visit *https://kdp.kseacademy.com/writing-b1-book* for more information. Use the coupon *AMZWB1* for a great discount as a thank you for purchasing this book.

Part 2

Choose **one** of these questions.

Write your answer in about **100 words** on the answer sheet.

Question 2

You see this notice on an English-language website.

READING

Do you love to read?

What are some of your favorite books or genres and why?

Where do you like to go in town to find new books to read?

Write an article and publish it on our website.

Write your **article**.

Question 3

Your English teacher has asked you to write a story.

Your story must begin with this sentence:

Tom realised he had forgotten his keys.

Write your **story**.

Do you need someone to mark your writing tasks?

Check out KSE Academy's writing assessment service. Scan the QR code on the left with your phone or visit *https://kdp.kseacademy.com/writing-b1-book* for more information. Use the coupon *AMZWB1* for a great discount as a thank you for purchasing this book.

THIS PAGE IS PHOTOCOPIABLE

Sample
Test 5

PRELIMINARY ENGLISH TEST

Writing

Time   45 minutes

INSTRUCTIONS TO CANDIDATES

Do not open this question paper until you are told to do so.

Write your name, centre number and candidate number on your answer sheet if they are not already there.

Read the instructions for each part of the paper carefully.

Answer the Part 1 question and one question from Part 2.

Write your answers on the answer sheet.

Write clearly in **pen**, not pencil. You may make alterations, but make sure your work is easy to read.

You **must** complete the answer sheet within the time limit.

At the end of the test, hand in both this question paper and your answer sheet.

INFORMATION FOR CANDIDATES

Each question in this paper carries equal marks.

Part 1

You **must** answer this question.

Write your answer in about **100 words** on the answer sheet.

Question 1

Read this email from your English-speaking friend Vicky and the notes you have made.

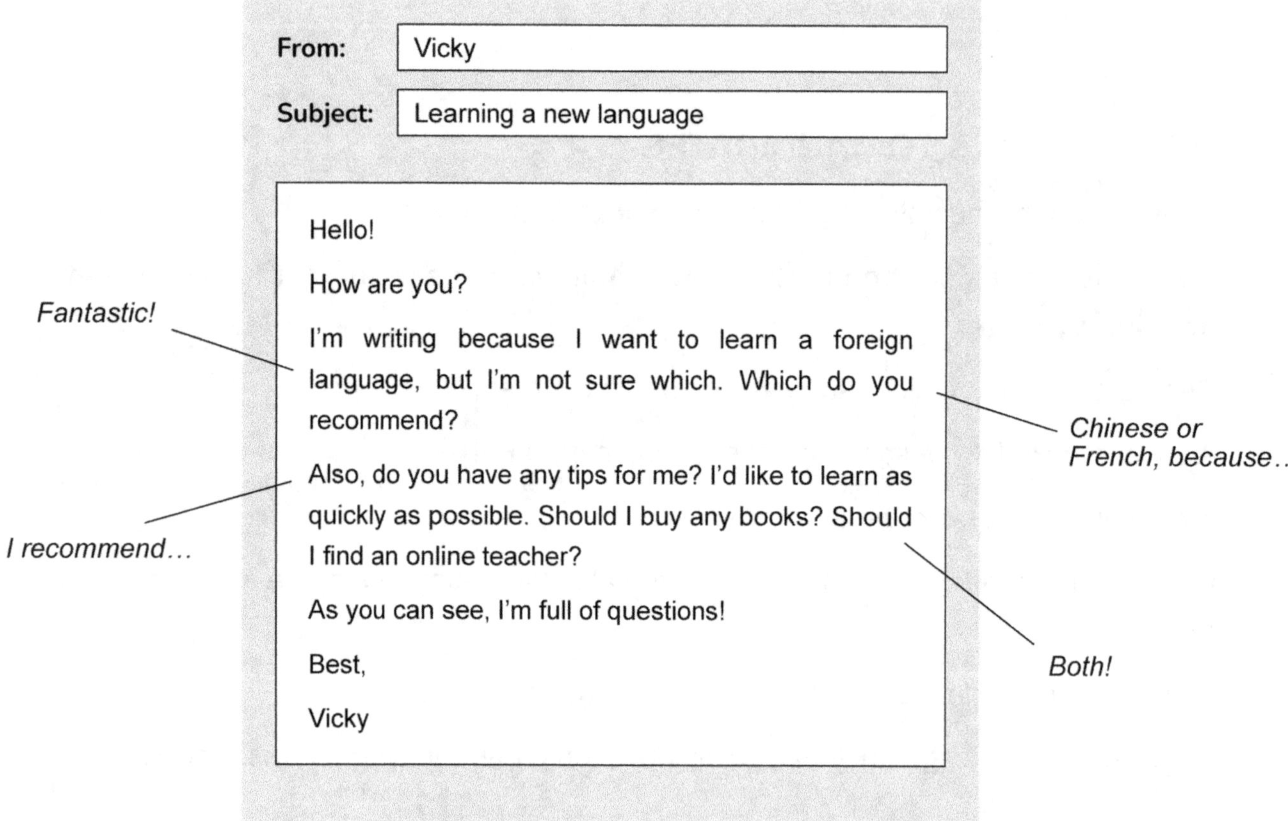

Write your **email** to Vicky using **all the notes**.

Do you need someone to mark your writing tasks?

Check out KSE Academy's writing assessment service. Scan the QR code on the left with your phone or visit *https://kdp.kseacademy.com/writing-b1-book* for more information. Use the coupon *AMZWB1* for a great discount as a thank you for purchasing this book.

Part 2

Choose **one** of these questions.

Write your answer in about **100 words** on the answer sheet.

Question 2

You see this notice in a local English-language newspaper.

WATER SPORTS

Do you prefer the sea or the swimming pool?

What are some of your favorite water sports to do in town?

What are the best places in town to go for water sports?

Write an article for the readers of our local newspaper.

Write your **article**.

Question 3

Your English teacher has asked you to write a story.

Your story must begin with this sentence:

Emily was smiling when she got off the plane.

Write your **story**.

Do you need someone to mark your writing tasks?

Check out KSE Academy's writing assessment service. Scan the QR code on the left with your phone or visit *https://kdp.kseacademy.com/writing-b1-book* for more information. Use the coupon *AMZWB1* for a great discount as a thank you for purchasing this book.

More Cambridge resources by the Author

Writing books

Writing for B2 and C1

These guides cover the main writing tasks that appear in the Cambridge English tests called B2 First (FCE) and C1 Advanced (CAE). These books provide several sample tasks for each type of writing, plus more than 500 useful phrases that candidates can use in their writings for B2 First and C1 Advanced.

Get your digital copies at **shop.kseacademy.com**.

Use of English books

Use of English for B2 and C1 levels

These books contain ten practice tests for the Use of English of the C1 Advanced and B2 First tests. Whether you are a teacher or a student, you can benefit from the exercises in this book, as they will help you become familiar with the format and level of the exam, and the type of questions.

Get your digital copies at **shop.kseacademy.com**.

Speaking Series by Prosperity Education

In this series, Luis Porras Wadley and Prosperity Education join forces to bring you 10 Speaking practice tests for the different examination levels. Get your digital copies now at **prosperityeducation.net**.

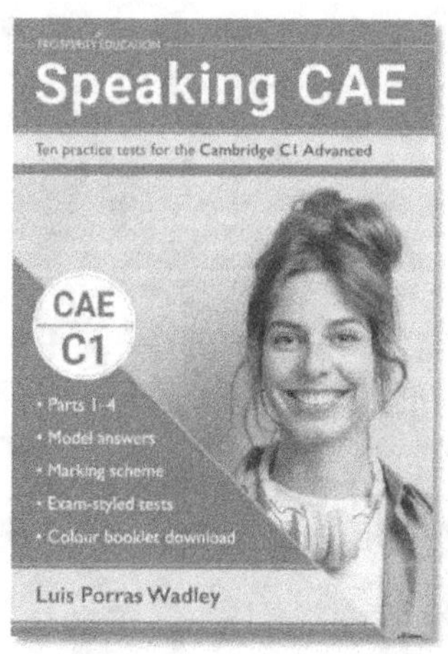

Extras & Freebies

Need help with your writing tasks?

Check out KSE Academy's writing assessment service. Scan the QR code on the left with your phone or visit *https://kdp.kseacademy.com/writing-b1-book* for more information. Use the coupon *AMZWB1* for a great discount as a thank you for purchasing this book.

Download more freebies

Scan the QR code below or visit *https://kdp.kseacademy.com/b1-writing-freebies* and download free resources for B1 Preliminary (PET). These are useful B1 Preliminary resources for people preparing for this Cambridge examination.